Lives and Times

W. K. Kellogg

Tiffany Peterson

Heinemann Library
Chicago, Illinois

© 2003 Heinemann Library
a division of Reed Elsevier Inc.
Chicago, Illinois

Customer Service 888-454-2279

Visit our website at www.heinemannlibrary.com

Designed by Herman Adler Design
Printed and bound in China by South China Printing Company
07 06 05
10 9 8 7 6 5 4 3 2

Library of Congress Cataloging-in-Publication Data
Peterson, Tiffany.
  W.K. Kellogg / Tiffany Peterson.
      p. cm. -- (Lives and times)
Summary: Introduces the life of W.K. Kellogg, who invented cold cereal, founded the company that makes much of the cereal in the United States, and established a foundation to help people.
Includes bibliographical references and index.
  ISBN 1-4034-3249-X (hardcover, library binding) -- ISBN 1-4034-4259-2 (pbk.)

1. Kellogg, W. K. (Will Keith), 1860-1951--Juvenile literature. 2. Industrialists--United States--Biography--Juvenile literature. 3. Philanthropists--United States--Biography--Juvenile literature. 4. Cereal products industry--United States--History--Juvenile literature. 5. Kellogg Company--History--Juvenile literature. [1. Kellogg, W. K. (Will Keith), 1860-1951. 2. Industrialists. 3. Philanthropists. 4. Food Industry and trade. 5. Kellogg Company.] I. Title. II. Lives and times (Des Plaines, Ill.)
  HD9056.U6K457 2003
  338.7'6647'092--dc21

2003001521

Acknowledgments
The author and publishers are grateful to the following for permission to reproduce copyright material:
Unless otherwise noted images provided by Kellogg Company, Kellogg's Cereal City, USA, and W. K. Kellogg Foundation. Used with permission.

Cover, pp. 1, 4 Brian Warling/Heinemann Library.

Photo research by Carol Parden.

Special thanks to Michelle Rimsa for her comments in the preparation of this book.

Some words are shown in bold, **like this.** You can find out what they mean by looking in the glossary.

Contents

Cereal for Breakfast

Cold cereal is a popular breakfast food. You may have had it for breakfast this morning. Kellogg's makes much of the cereal in the United States.

Kellogg's brand cereals come in a wide variety of flavors.

4

Cereal flakes were **invented** by chance in the late 1800s. Will Keith (W. K.) Kellogg and his brother John Harvey made them.

W. K. was working for his brother when they made the first wheat-flake cereal.

The Early Years

W. K. helped on his father's farm every day after school. In this family photo, W. K. is the child in the center.

W. K. Kellogg was born on April 7, 1860, in Battle Creek, Michigan. He did not do very well in school. He could not see the **blackboard** because he needed glasses.

When he was fourteen, W. K. left school. He became a salesperson for his father's broom company. He became a good businessperson.

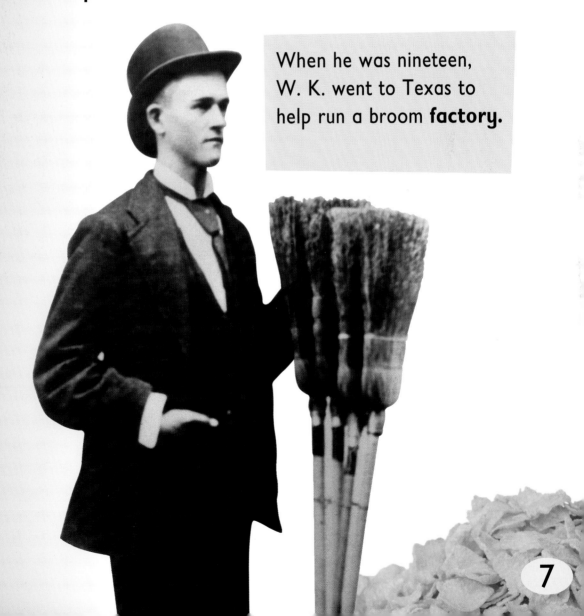

When he was nineteen, W. K. went to Texas to help run a broom **factory**.

A Return Home and a Wedding

W. K. worked in Texas for one year. In 1879, he returned to Michigan and married Ella Osborn Davis. She had also grown up in Battle Creek.

W. K. had known Ella for many years before they got married.

W. K. was often home only when his children were sleeping. Elizabeth, John, and Karl are shown here.

W. K. and his wife had four sons and a daughter. W. K. worked long hours, so he did not have much time to spend with his family.

A New Job

W. K. went to work for his brother, John Harvey. John Harvey was a doctor and ran a **sanitorium.** The sanitorium was a hospital and a vacation spot.

People who stayed at the sanitorium called it the San.

W. K. handled the money for the San. He also did small jobs, such as shining John Harvey's shoes. W. K. worked hard, but he was unhappy with his job.

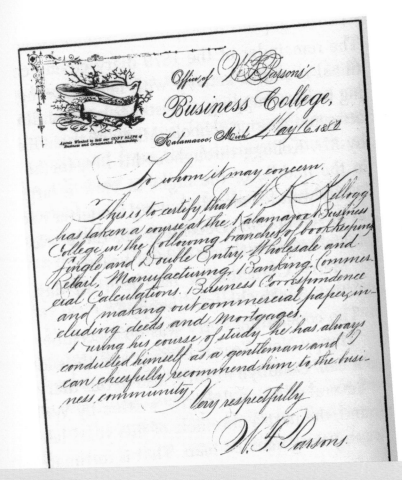

W. K. wanted to be successful, so he went to business school. This is the **certificate** they gave him.

Breakfast Foods

The San did not serve tea, coffee, or **spicy** food.

John Harvey served simple foods at the San. Patients did not like the taste of it, though. So, John Harvey asked W. K. to help him find a tasty, healthful breakfast food.

12

By chance, W. K. left a pot of boiled wheat sitting for two days. When the brothers rolled out the mushy wheat, it came out in flakes. When toasted, the flakes tasted quite good.

This museum display shows W. K. and John Harvey on the day they made wheat flakes.

A New Business

John Harvey served the toasted wheat flakes for breakfast at the San. People liked this new food. People even wanted to eat the cereal at home.

The Kellogg brothers sold their cereal through the San's food company, Sanitas.

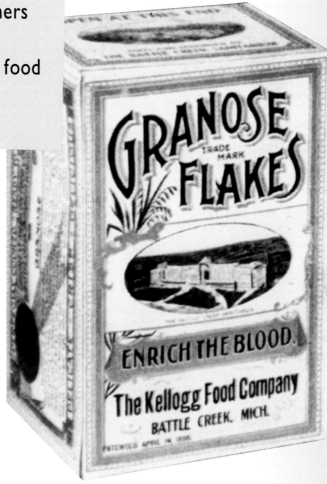

14

People who had never been to the San began ordering the cereal.

W. K. was put in charge of his brother's new food business. He worked hard to make the business grow. He **advertised** in newspapers and magazines.

On His Own

W. K. **experimented** to make the cereal better. He used corn instead of wheat. Then he added a little sugar.

W. K. found that sugar made corn or wheat flakes taste better.

John Harvey did not want to add sugar to food. So, W. K. started his own company. It was called the Battle Creek Toasted Corn Flake Company.

W. K. opened his first **factory** in 1906 on Brook Street, behind the San.

Other Cereals

The Kelloggs had gotten people interested in cereal. During the early 1900s, more than 40 companies in Battle Creek were selling wheat-flake cereal.

Battle Creek, Michigan, became known as the cereal capital of the world.

One of these other companies was successful. C. W. Post had stayed at the San. He liked Kellogg's cereal so much that he started his own cereal company.

Post's company, Post Cereal, still makes **cornflakes.**

Success!

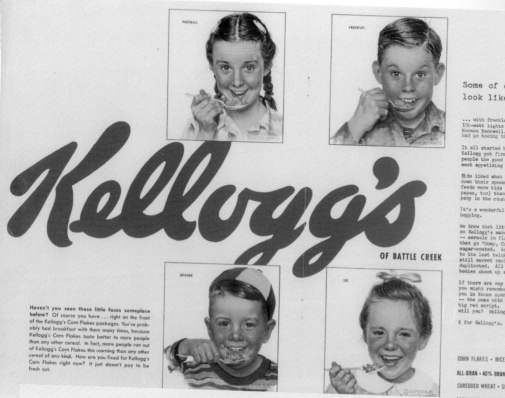

Some of our best customers look like this

... with freckles and hair ribbons and beanies and 150-watt lights in the eyes, as captured here by Norman Rockwell. Kids! The little people who've had us toeing the mark now for nearly 50 years.

It all started back in 1906. That's when Mr. W. K. Kellogg got fired up with the idea of bringing people the good and wholesome grains in a new and most appetizing form.

Kids liked what they tasted and they've never laid down their spoons. Today and every day, Kellogg's feeds more kids (and of course, more mamas and papas, too) than any other ready-to-eat cereal company in the country.

It's a wonderful responsibility, that keeps us hopping.

We know that little appetites need to be coaxed, so Kellogg's makes everything to coax them with — cereals in flakes, in puffs, in shreds. Some that go "Snap, Crackle, Pop." Some that are even sugar-coated. And all toasted in our radiant ovens to the last twinkle of freshness. All made to our still secret recipes with flavor that's never been duplicated. All rich in the stuff that makes little bodies shoot up and blossom and thrive.

If there are any little spooner-uppers at your house, you might remember that this is what's waiting for you in those spanking, sparkling Kellogg's packages — the ones with Mr. Kellogg's original signature in big red script. Don't ever settle for less, now, will you? Kellogg's, that's the name to reach for.

K for Kellogg's. K for kids.

CORN FLAKES · RICE KRISPIES · PEP WHEAT FLAKES

ALL-BRAN · 40% BRAN FLAKES · RAISIN BRAN · SUGAR CORN POPS

SHREDDED WHEAT · SUGAR SMACKS · SUGAR FROSTED FLAKES

CORN SOYA · KRUMBLES · VARIETY · SNACK-PAK · HANDI-PAK

Haven't you seen these little faces someplace before? Of course you have ... right on the front of the Kellogg's Corn Flakes packages. You've probably had breakfast with them many times, because Kellogg's Corn Flakes taste better to more people than any other cereal. In fact, more people ran out of Kellogg's Corn Flakes this morning than any other cereal of any kind. How are you fixed for Kellogg's Corn Flakes right now? It just doesn't pay to be fresh out.

Some ads offered free cereal to anyone who asked for Kellogg's cereal at a store.

W. K. had to get people to buy his cereal instead of the **imitations.** He knew the key was getting stores to sell it. He turned to **advertising.**

W. K.'s advertisements were a success. Toasted **Corn Flakes** were soon being sold in stores all around the country.

The name Sanitas was replaced with Kellogg's in 1907.

A Friendly Boss

W. K. was a good boss. He wanted people to work hard, but he treated them well. When his **factory** burned down in 1907, W. K. kept paying his workers.

W. K. paid his workers to help clean up and rebuild the factory.

W. K. often toured his cereal factory to visit the workers. He also tested new equipment.

If W. K. heard that one of his workers could not pay for a doctor, he would secretly pay the bill himself.

Caring for Others

W. K.'s wife, Ella, died in 1912. W. K. was alone for the next six years. He kept working on making better cereal. Six years later, he married his second wife.

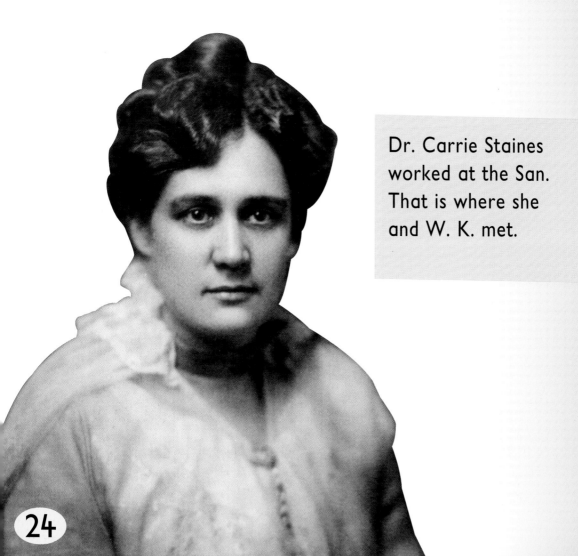

Dr. Carrie Staines worked at the San. That is where she and W. K. met.

W. K.'s company made him rich. He used his money to help people. He gave money for poor children to go see doctors. He also built schools and summer camps.

Summer camps such as this one near Battle Creek were for poor children.

A Special School

The Kellogg school was the first to have regular and special education students together.

W. K. started the Ann J. Kellogg School, named for his mother. Any child could go to the school. Some children at the school had trouble seeing, hearing, or walking.

In his mid-60s, W. K. learned he had an eye illness called **glaucoma.** By 1942, he was blind. W. K. died on October 6, 1951. He was 91 years old.

W. K.'s guide dog helped him move around on his own.

Learning More About W. K. Kellogg

W. K. Kellogg is remembered not only as the **inventor** of cereal flakes. He is also remembered as a very giving man.

At the Cereal City USA museum in Battle Creek, visitors can learn more about W. K. Kellogg's life.

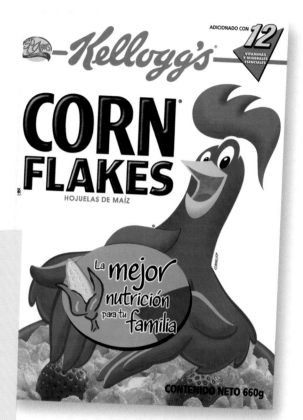

Kellogg's products are sold in 160 countries. The labeling on this box is in Spanish.

Today, Kellogg's is the world's top cereal maker. The company has **factories** in nineteen countries. The W. K. Kellogg Foundation continues W. K.'s work in helping people.

Fact File

- W. K. took steps to help protect wildlife and the environment as well as working with people.

- The main office of the Kellogg's Company is still in Battle Creek, Michigan.

- At the Michigan Historical Museum in Lansing, Michigan, visitors can learn more about the cereal boom in Battle Creek.

- All his life, W. K. liked horses. He built a place in California where he kept 30 horses.

Timeline

April 7, 1860 W. K. Kellogg is born in Battle Creek, Michigan

1880 W. K. marries Ella Osborn Davis and goes to work for his brother at the San

1894 W. K. and his brother discover how to make wheat flakes

1906 W. K. starts his own cereal business—the Battle Creek Toasted Corn Flake Company

1912 Ella Osborn Kellogg dies

1918 W. K. marries Dr. Carrie Staines

October 6, 1951 W. K. Kellogg dies

Glossary

advertise to tell people about something so they will buy it

blackboard board at the front of a classroom, on which a teacher writes with chalk

certificate official letter that says someone has completed school

cornflakes cold cereal made from corn that has been cooked and rolled into flakes

experiment to test in order to discover or prove something

factory place where a large amount of something is made

glaucoma sickness of the eye that can cause blindness

imitation fake; something that copies something else

invent make something that has never been made before

sanitorium hospital

signature a person's name written in his or her own handwriting

spicy having a strong flavor

More Books to Read

Frost, Helen. *The Grain Group*. Mankato, Minn.: Capstone, 2000.

McGrath, Barbara Barbieri. *Kellogg's Froot Loops Color Fun Book*. New York: HarperCollins, 2001.

An older reader can help you with this book:

Epstein, Rachel. *W. K. Kellogg: Generous Genius*. New York: Children's Press, 2000.

Index